Applying the Standards:
STEM
Grade 4

Credits
Content Editor: Natalie Rompella
Copy Editor: Beatrice Allen

Visit *carsondellosa.com* for correlations to Common Core, state, national, and Canadian provincial standards.

Carson-Dellosa Publishing, LLC
PO Box 35665
Greensboro, NC 27425 USA
carsondellosa.com

ISBN 978-1-4838-1575-6
02-278151151

Table of Contents

Introduction

STEM education is a growing force in today's classroom. Exposure to science, technology, engineering, and math is important in twenty-first century learning as it allows students to succeed in higher education as well as a variety of careers.

While it can come in many forms, STEM education is most often presented as an engaging task that asks students to solve a problem. Additionally, creativity, collaboration, communication, and critical thinking are integral to every task. STEM projects are authentic learning tasks that guide students to address a variety of science and math standards. Also, students strengthen English Language Arts skills by recording notes and written reflections throughout the process.

In this book, students are asked to complete a range of tasks with limited resources. Materials for each task are limited to common household objects. Students are guided through each task by the steps of the engineering design process to provide a framework through which students can grow their comfort levels and independently complete tasks.

Use the included rubric to guide assessment of student responses and further plan any necessary remediation. Confidence in STEM tasks will help students succeed in their school years and beyond.

Student Roles

Student collaboration is an important component of STEM learning. Encourage collaboration by having students complete tasks in groups. Teach students to communicate openly, support each other, and respect the contributions of all members. Keep in mind that collaborative grouping across achievement levels can provide benefits for all students as they pool various perspectives and experiences toward a group goal.

Consider assigning formal roles to students in each group. This will simplify the collaborative tasks needed to get a project done and done well. The basic roles of group structure are as follows:

- The *captain* leads and guides other students in their roles.

- The *guide* walks the team through the steps, keeps track of time, and encourages the team to try again.

- The *materials manager* gathers, organizes, and guides the use of materials.

- The *reporter* records the team's thoughts and reports on the final project to the class.

STEM Performance Rubric

Use this rubric as a guide for assessing students' project management skills. It can also be offered to students as a tool to show your expectations and scoring. Note: Some items may not apply to each project.

4
- _____ Asks or identifies comprehensive high-level questions
- _____ Exhibits impressive imagination and creativity
- _____ Uses an appropriate, complete strategy to solve the problem
- _____ Skillfully justifies the solution and strategy used
- _____ Offers insightful reasoning and strong evidence of critical thinking
- _____ Collaborates with others in each stage of the process
- _____ Effectively evaluates and organizes information and outcomes

3
- _____ Asks or identifies ample high-level questions
- _____ Exhibits effective imagination and creativity
- _____ Uses an appropriate but incomplete strategy to solve the problem
- _____ Justifies answer and strategy used
- _____ Offers sufficient reasoning and evidence of critical thinking
- _____ Collaborates with others in most stages of the process
- _____ Evaluates and organizes some information or outcomes

2
- _____ Asks or identifies a few related questions
- _____ Exhibits little imagination and creativity
- _____ Uses an inappropriate or unclear strategy for solving the problem
- _____ Attempts to justify answers and strategy used
- _____ Demonstrates some evidence of critical thinking
- _____ Collaborates with others if prompted
- _____ Can evaluate and organize simple information or outcomes

1
- _____ Is unable to ask or identify pertinent questions
- _____ Does not exhibit adequate imagination and creativity
- _____ Uses no strategy or plan for solving the problem
- _____ Does not or cannot justify answer or strategy used
- _____ Demonstrates limited or no evidence of critical thinking
- _____ Does not collaborate with others
- _____ Cannot evaluate or organize information or outcomes

Name _____

Read the task. Then, follow the steps to complete the task.

Paper Pals: Engineering

Using only folded paper and scissors, create at least 2 paper people linked together.

Materials

large sheet of paper   scissors

Ask

What do you already know? What do you need to know to get started? Where can you find the information you need?

_____

_____

_____

Imagine

What are the possibilities? Come up with several different options.

_____

_____

Plan

Choose an idea. Draw a model and label it. Consider making different models for each stage of construction or separate diagrams of more complex parts.

📝 Plan

What are your steps? Use your drawing to guide your plan. Number your steps and write clearly so that others can understand them.

_____

_____

_____

🛠️ Create

Follow your plan to create your model. What worked? What didn't? What did you need to change as you went through your plan? Why?

_____

_____

_____

🔄 Improve

How could you improve your model? Do you need to start over, or can you redo a single part? If it works, can it work even better?

_____

_____

_____

💬 Communicate

How well did it work? Is the problem solved? Write a statement to describe how your model meets the guidelines of the task and why it is successful.

_____

_____

_____

☀️ Reflect

What are tips you would give others on how to keep the paper people connected?

_____

_____

_____

_____

Name _____

Read the task. Then, follow the steps to complete the task.

Juicy Combos: Chemistry

Create a new combination of juices for people to enjoy.

Materials

a variety of prepared
   juices, such as
   cranberry and orange
   juices
drinking cups

measuring cups and
   spoons
seltzer water
club soda
water

Caution: Before beginning any food activity, ask families' permission and inquire about students' food allergies and religious or other food restrictions.

Ask

What do you already know? What do you need to know to get started? Where can you find the information you need?

_____

_____

_____

Imagine

What are the possibilities? Come up with several different options.

_____

_____

Plan

Choose an idea. Draw a model and label it. Consider making different models for each stage of construction or separate diagrams of more complex parts.

📓 Plan

What are your steps? Use your drawing to guide your plan. Number your steps and write clearly so that others can understand them.

_____

_____

_____

🛠️ Create

Follow your plan to create your model. What worked? What didn't? What did you need to change as you went through your plan? Why?

_____

_____

_____

🔄 Improve

How could you improve your model? Do you need to start over, or can you redo a single part? If it works, can it work even better?

_____

_____

_____

💬 Communicate

How well did it work? Is the problem solved? Write a statement to describe how your model meets the guidelines of the task and why it is successful.

_____

_____

_____

☀️ Reflect

In fractions, tell how many parts each you used of juice, water, seltzer water, or club soda to make a winning combination.

_____

_____

_____

Name _____

Read the task. Then, follow the steps to complete the task.

Don't Pop the Present: Geometry

Neatly gift wrap a balloon with a single sheet of paper.

Materials

large sheet of paper or   scissors
   wrapping paper   tape
balloon

Caution: Before beginning any balloon activity, ask families about possible latex allergies. Also, remember that uninflated or popped balloons may present a choking hazard.

Ask

What do you already know? What do you need to know to get started? Where can you find the information you need?

_____

_____

_____

Imagine

What are the possibilities? Come up with several different options.

_____

_____

_____

Plan

Choose an idea. Draw a model and label it. Consider making different models for each stage of construction or separate diagrams of more complex parts.

📝 Plan

What are your steps? Use your drawing to guide your plan. Number your steps and write clearly so that others can understand them.

_____

_____

_____

🔧 Create

Follow your plan to create your model. What worked? What didn't? What did you need to change as you went through your plan? Why?

_____

_____

_____

🔄 Improve

How could you improve your model? Do you need to start over, or can you redo a single part? If it works, can it work even better?

_____

_____

_____

💬 Communicate

How well did it work? Is the problem solved? Write a statement to describe how your model meets the guidelines of the task and why it is successful.

_____

_____

_____

☀️ Reflect

What paper shape worked best? Why?

_____

_____

_____

_____

Name _____

Read the task. Then, follow the steps to complete the task.

Cardboard Car: Building and Design

Using a toilet paper tube, create a car that can roll 1 foot (30 cm).

Materials

any items you choose,   glue
   such as cardboard,   pencil
   straws, and thread   ruler or meterstick
   spools   scissors
toilet paper tube   tape

Ask

What do you already know? What do you need to know to get started? Where can you find the information you need?

_____

_____

_____

Imagine

What are the possibilities? Come up with several different options.

_____

_____

_____

Plan

Choose an idea. Draw a model and label it. Consider making different models for each stage of construction or separate diagrams of more complex parts.

Plan

What are your steps? Use your drawing to guide your plan. Number your steps and write clearly so that others can understand them.

_____

_____

_____

_____

Create

Follow your plan to create your model. What worked? What didn't? What did you need to change as you went through your plan? Why?

_____

_____

_____

Improve

How could you improve your model? Do you need to start over, or can you redo a single part? If it works, can it work even better?

_____

_____

_____

Communicate

How well did it work? Is the problem solved? Write a statement to describe how your model meets the guidelines of the task and why it is successful.

_____

_____

_____

Reflect

What features are important to include for any kind of toy car you would create?

_____

_____

_____

_____

Name _____

Read the task. Then, follow the steps to complete the task.

Hole in One: Physics

Design a miniature-golf hole.

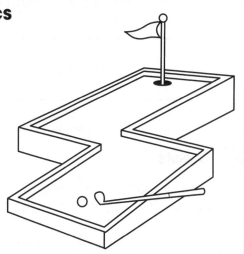

Materials

any items you choose, such as cardboard tubes, empty boxes, felt, and large sheets of cardboard

golf ball

tape

putter (can be homemade, such as a wrapping paper tube with cardboard taped to the end)

glue

scissors

 Ask

What do you already know? What do you need to know to get started? Where can you find the information you need?

_____

_____

_____

Imagine

What are the possibilities? Come up with several different options.

_____

_____

_____

Plan

Choose an idea. Draw a model and label it. Consider making different models for each stage of construction or separate diagrams of more complex parts.

✍️ Plan

What are your steps? Use your drawing to guide your plan. Number your steps and write clearly so that others can understand them.

_____

_____

_____

_____

✂️ Create

Follow your plan to create your model. What worked? What didn't? What did you need to change as you went through your plan? Why?

_____

_____

_____

🔄 Improve

How could you improve your model? Do you need to start over, or can you redo a single part? If it works, can it work even better?

_____

_____

_____

💬 Communicate

How well did it work? Is the problem solved? Write a statement to describe how your model meets the guidelines of the task and why it is successful.

_____

_____

_____

☀️ Reflect

What elements of science—such as gravity, friction, or magnetism—did you use to create your hole?

_____

_____

_____

_____

Name _____

Read the task. Then, follow the steps to complete the task.

Pulley with a Purpose: Simple Machines

Create a pulley that can lift a paper cup.

Materials

small paper cup	yarn or string
pencil	empty spools
surface to hang the pulley from, such as a tall box, a stairway, or a table	paper clip
	scissors
	tape

Ask

What do you already know? What do you need to know to get started? Where can you find the information you need?

_____

_____

_____

Imagine

What are the possibilities? Come up with several different options.

_____

_____

_____

Plan

Choose an idea. Draw a model and label it. Consider making different models for each stage of construction or separate diagrams of more complex parts.

📝 Plan

What are your steps? Use your drawing to guide your plan. Number your steps and write clearly so that others can understand them.

_____

_____

_____

_____

🛠 Create

Follow your plan to create your model. What worked? What didn't? What did you need to change as you went through your plan? Why?

_____

_____

_____

🔄 Improve

How could you improve your model? Do you need to start over, or can you redo a single part? If it works, can it work even better?

_____

_____

_____

💬 Communicate

How well did it work? Is the problem solved? Write a statement to describe how your model meets the guidelines of the task and why it is successful.

_____

_____

_____

☀ Reflect

In real life, where might someone need to use a pulley?

_____

_____

_____

Name _____

Read the task. Then, follow the steps to complete the task.

Need a Ride?

Figure out a way to move a toy car without touching it.

Materials

any items you choose,   toy car
  such as dominoes,
  magnets, and straws

Ask

What do you already know? What do you need to know to get started? Where can you find the information you need?

_____

_____

_____

Imagine

What are the possibilities? Come up with several different options.

_____

_____

_____

Plan

Choose an idea. Draw a model and label it. Consider making different models for each stage of construction or separate diagrams of more complex parts.

Plan

What are your steps? Use your drawing to guide your plan. Number your steps and write clearly so that others can understand them.

_____

_____

_____

_____

Create

Follow your plan to create your model. What worked? What didn't? What did you need to change as you went through your plan? Why?

_____

_____

_____

Improve

How could you improve your model? Do you need to start over, or can you redo a single part? If it works, can it work even better?

_____

_____

_____

Communicate

How well did it work? Is the problem solved? Write a statement to describe how your model meets the guidelines of the task and why it is successful.

_____

_____

_____

Reflect

What other supplies would have been helpful? Why?

_____

_____

_____

_____

   © Carson-Dellosa · CD-104855 · Applying the Standards: STEM

Name _____

Read the task. Then, follow the steps to complete the task.

Say Cheese! Exploring Light

Take a picture of a friend so that your friend is in silhouette (in shadow in front of a light background).

Materials

digital camera   friend or object

Ask

What do you already know? What do you need to know to get started? Where can you find the information you need?

_____

_____

_____

Imagine

What are the possibilities? Come up with several different options.

_____

_____

_____

Plan

Choose an idea. Draw a model and label it. Consider making different models for each stage of construction or separate diagrams of more complex parts.

📝 Plan

What are your steps? Use your drawing to guide your plan. Number your steps and write clearly so that others can understand them.

_____

_____

_____

_____

🛠️ Create

Follow your plan to create your model. What worked? What didn't? What did you need to change as you went through your plan? Why?

_____

_____

_____

🔄 Improve

How could you improve your model? Do you need to start over, or can you redo a single part? If it works, can it work even better?

_____

_____

_____

💬 Communicate

How well did it work? Is the problem solved? Write a statement to describe how your model meets the guidelines of the task and why it is successful.

_____

_____

_____

☀️ Reflect

What are some tips you learned that would help you take a picture that clearly shows the person's face rather than a silhouette?

_____

_____

_____

Name _____

Read the task. Then, follow the steps to complete the task.

Wind Wheel: Combining Design and Wind Power

Create a pinwheel that spins in the wind.

Materials

stick, such as a pencil,
   skewer, or wooden
   dowel
variety of paper, such as
   cardboard, card stock,
   and computer paper

brass fasteners
glue
hole punch
pushpins
tape
scissors

Caution: Before beginning any outdoor activity, ask families' permission and recommend use of sunscreen and/or sun-protective clothing.

Ask

What do you already know? What do you need to know to get started? Where can you find the information you need?

_____

_____

_____

Imagine

What are the possibilities? Come up with several different options.

_____

_____

_____

Plan

Choose an idea. Draw a model and label it. Consider making different models for each stage of construction or separate diagrams of more complex parts.

Plan

What are your steps? Use your drawing to guide your plan. Number your steps and write clearly so that others can understand them.

Create

Follow your plan to create your model. What worked? What didn't? What did you need to change as you went through your plan? Why?

Improve

How could you improve your model? Do you need to start over, or can you redo a single part? If it works, can it work even better?

Communicate

How well did it work? Is the problem solved? Write a statement to describe how your model meets the guidelines of the task and why it is successful.

Reflect

How could you get your pinwheel to spin in the opposite direction?

Name _____

Read the task. Then, follow the steps to complete the task.

Puddle Predicament

Find a way to measure the water in a puddle.

Materials

graduated cylinder   paper
measuring cups   pencil
ruler   paper towels

Caution: Before beginning any outdoor activity, ask families' permission and recommend use of sunscreen and/or sun-protective clothing.

Ask

What do you already know? What do you need to know to get started? Where can you find the information you need?

_____

_____

_____

Imagine

What are the possibilities? Come up with several different options.

_____

_____

_____

Plan

Choose an idea. Draw a model and label it. Consider making different models for each stage of construction or separate diagrams of more complex parts.

Plan

What are your steps? Use your drawing to guide your plan. Number your steps and write clearly so that others can understand them.

_____

_____

_____

Create

Follow your plan to create your model. What worked? What didn't? What did you need to change as you went through your plan? Why?

_____

_____

_____

Improve

How could you improve your model? Do you need to start over, or can you redo a single part? If it works, can it work even better?

_____

_____

_____

Communicate

How well did it work? Is the problem solved? Write a statement to describe how your model meets the guidelines of the task and why it is successful.

_____

_____

_____

Reflect

What unit of measurement did you use? Why?

_____

_____

_____

_____

Name _____

Read the task. Then, follow the steps to complete the task.

Paper 'Scraper: Engineering

Create the tallest structure you can using only paper and tape.

Materials

variety of paper, such   tape
as old newspapers or   scissors
recycled computer
paper

Ask

What do you already know? What do you need to know to get started? Where can you find the information you need?

_____

_____

_____

Imagine

What are the possibilities? Come up with several different options.

_____

_____

_____

Plan

Choose an idea. Draw a model and label it. Consider making different models for each stage of construction or separate diagrams of more complex parts.

📓 Plan

What are your steps? Use your drawing to guide your plan. Number your steps and write clearly so that others can understand them.

_____

_____

_____

_____

🛠️ Create

Follow your plan to create your model. What worked? What didn't? What did you need to change as you went through your plan? Why?

_____

_____

_____

🔄 Improve

How could you improve your model? Do you need to start over, or can you redo a single part? If it works, can it work even better?

_____

_____

_____

💬 Communicate

How well did it work? Is the problem solved? Write a statement to describe how your model meets the guidelines of the task and why it is successful.

_____

_____

_____

☀️ Reflect

What shapes helped make your design strong? How was shape a factor?

_____

_____

_____

_____

Name _____

Read the task. Then, follow the steps to complete the task.

Clear It Up: Water Filtration

Create a filter to clean dirty water.

Materials

any items you choose,
    such as coffee filters,
    paper towels, pebbles,
    rocks, and sand
dirty water (can be made
    mixing water and soil)

empty soda or water
    bottle with the bottom
    cut off
clear plastic cup
tape
craft sticks

Caution: Before beginning this activity, remind students that the water is for project use only.

Ask

What do you already know? What do you need to know to get started? Where can you find the information you need?

_____

_____

_____

Imagine

What are the possibilities? Come up with several different options.

_____

_____

_____

Plan

Choose an idea. Draw a model and label it. Consider making different models for each stage of construction or separate diagrams of more complex parts.

✎ Plan

What are your steps? Use your drawing to guide your plan. Number your steps and write clearly so others can understand them.

_____

_____

_____

✂ Create

Follow your plan to create your model. What worked? What didn't? What did you need to change as you went through your plan? Why?

_____

_____

_____

⟳ Improve

How could you improve your model? Do you need to start over, or can you redo a single part? If it works, can it work even better?

_____

_____

_____

💬 Communicate

How well did it work? Is the problem solved? Write a statement to describe how your model meets the guidelines of the task and why it is successful.

_____

_____

_____

☀ Reflect

In nature, what filters water? Give several different examples.

_____

_____

_____

_____

Name _____

Read the task. Then, follow the steps to complete the task.

High-Flying Marshmallows: Building a Catapult

Make a marshmallow catapult.

Materials

any items you choose,
    such as chenille stems,
    empty boxes, pencils,
    rubber bands, plastic
    spoons, string, and
    craft sticks

large marshmallows

Ask

What do you already know? What do you need to know to get started? Where can you find the information you need?

_____

_____

_____

Imagine

What are the possibilities? Come up with several different options.

_____

_____

_____

Plan

Choose an idea. Draw a model and label it. Consider making different models for each stage of construction or separate diagrams of more complex parts.

Plan

What are your steps? Use your drawing to guide your plan. Number your steps and write clearly so others can understand them.

_____

_____

_____

_____

Create

Follow your plan to create your model. What worked? What didn't? What did you need to change as you went through your plan? Why?

_____

_____

_____

Improve

How could you improve your model? Do you need to start over, or can you redo a single part? If it works, can it work even better?

_____

_____

_____

Communicate

How well did it work? Is the problem solved? Write a statement to describe how your model meets the guidelines of the task and why it is successful.

_____

_____

_____

Reflect

How can you change the trajectory, or path, of the marshmallows?

_____

_____

_____

_____

Name _____

Read the task. Then, follow the steps to complete the task.

Outdoor Clock: Building a Sundial

Design a sundial that can accurately show the time.

Materials

sunlight	pencil
paper plates	clay

Caution: Before beginning any outdoor activity, ask families' permission and recommend use of sunscreen and/or sun-protective clothing.

🔑 Ask

What do you already know? What do you need to know to get started? Where can you find the information you need?

_____

_____

_____

☁ Imagine

What are the possibilities? Come up with several different options.

_____

_____

_____

📓 Plan

Choose an idea. Draw a model and label it. Consider making different models for each stage of construction or separate diagrams of more complex parts.

Plan

What are your steps? Use your drawing to guide your plan. Number your steps and write clearly so others can understand them.

_____

_____

_____

Create

Follow your plan to create your model. What worked? What didn't? What did you need to change as you went through your plan? Why?

_____

_____

_____

Improve

How could you improve your model? Do you need to start over, or can you redo a single part? If it works, can it work even better?

_____

_____

_____

Communicate

How well did it work? Is the problem solved? Write a statement to describe how your model meets the guidelines of the task and why it is successful.

_____

_____

_____

Reflect

What is the position of the sun in relation to the shadow on a sundial?

_____

_____

_____

_____

Name _____

Read the task. Then, follow the steps to complete the task.

Build a Better Bridge

Using wooden craft sticks, design a bridge that can hold up a textbook.

Materials

wooden craft sticks   textbook
glue or a hot glue gun   paper
   (with help from an   pencil
   adult)

Caution: Use of a hot glue gun will require adult supervision.

Ask

What do you already know? What do you need to know to get started? Where can you find the information you need?

_____

_____

_____

Imagine

What are the possibilities? Come up with several different options.

_____

_____

_____

Plan

Choose an idea. Draw a model and label it. Consider making different models for each stage of construction or separate diagrams of more complex parts.

📓 Plan

What are your steps? Use your drawing to guide your plan. Number your steps and write clearly so others can understand them.

_____

_____

_____

_____

🛠 Create

Follow your plan to create your model. What worked? What didn't? What did you need to change as you went through your plan? Why?

_____

_____

_____

🔄 Improve

How could you improve your model? Do you need to start over, or can you redo a single part? If it works, can it work even better?

_____

_____

_____

💬 Communicate

How well did it work? Is the problem solved? Write a statement to describe how your model meets the guidelines of the task and why it is successful.

_____

_____

_____

☀ Reflect

What part(s) of your design added strength to your bridge? How?

_____

_____

_____

_____

Name _____

Read the task. Then, follow the steps to complete the task.

Dancing Marionette

Using a stuffed animal or soft doll, create a marionette that can dance.

Materials

stuffed animal or soft doll with moveable arms and legs	string
	tape or glue
	wooden craft sticks

Ask

What do you already know? What do you need to know to get started? Where can you find the information you need?

_____

_____

_____

Imagine

What are the possibilities? Come up with several different options.

_____

_____

_____

Plan

Choose an idea. Draw a model and label it. Consider making different models for each stage of construction or separate diagrams of more complex parts.

Plan

What are your steps? Use your drawing to guide your plan. Number your steps and write clearly so others can understand them.

_____

_____

_____

_____

Create

Follow your plan to create your model. What worked? What didn't? What did you need to change as you went through your plan? Why?

_____

_____

_____

Improve

How could you improve your model? Do you need to start over, or can you redo a single part? If it works, can it work even better?

_____

_____

_____

Communicate

How well did it work? Is the problem solved? Write a statement to describe how your model meets the guidelines of the task and why it is successful.

_____

_____

_____

Reflect

How does your design allow the marionette's legs to move?

_____

_____

_____

_____

Name _____

Read the task. Then, follow the steps to complete the task.

Sandal Sound-Off: Building and Design

Design and create a sandal that makes noise when you walk.

Materials

any items you choose, such as cardboard, empty boxes, string, rubber bands, and yarn	objects that can make noise, such as bells tape stapler glue

Ask

What do you already know? What do you need to know to get started? Where can you find the information you need?

_____

_____

_____

Imagine

What are the possibilities? Come up with several different options.

_____

_____

_____

Plan

Choose an idea. Draw a model and label it. Consider making different models for each stage of construction or separate diagrams of more complex parts.

📓 Plan

What are your steps? Use your drawing to guide your plan. Number your steps and write clearly so others can understand them.

_____

_____

_____

_____

🛠️ Create

Follow your plan to create your model. What worked? What didn't? What did you need to change as you went through your plan? Why?

_____

_____

_____

🔄 Improve

How could you improve your model? Do you need to start over, or can you redo a single part? If it works, can it work even better?

_____

_____

_____

💬 Communicate

How well did it work? Is the problem solved? Write a statement to describe how your model meets the guidelines of the task and why it is successful.

_____

_____

_____

☀️ Reflect

What was the most difficult part of your design to create?

_____

_____

_____

_____

Name _____

Read the task. Then, follow the steps to complete the task.

Balloon Movin'

Create a way to power a toy vehicle with a balloon.

Materials

any items you choose,
   such as paper, straws,
   and string
balloon

toy boat or toy car
scissors
tape
glue

Caution: Before beginning any balloon activity, ask families about possible latex allergies. Also, remember that uninflated or popped balloons may present a choking hazard.

Ask

What do you already know? What do you need to know to get started? Where can you find the information you need?

_____

_____

_____

Imagine

What are the possibilities? Come up with several different options.

_____

_____

_____

Plan

Choose an idea. Draw a model and label it. Consider making different models for each stage of construction or separate diagrams of more complex parts.

⬛ Plan

What are your steps? Use your drawing to guide your plan. Number your steps and write clearly so others can understand them.

_____

_____

_____

_____

⬛ Create

Follow your plan to create your model. What worked? What didn't? What did you need to change as you went through your plan? Why?

_____

_____

_____

⬛ Improve

How could you improve your model? Do you need to start over, or can you redo a single part? If it works, can it work even better?

_____

_____

_____

⬛ Communicate

How well did it work? Is the problem solved? Write a statement to describe how your model meets the guidelines of the task and why it is successful.

_____

_____

_____

⬛ Reflect

Where did you place the balloon in relation to your vehicle's motion? Explain your thinking.

_____

_____

_____

_____

Name _____

Read the task. Then, follow the steps to complete the task.

I Saw the Light: Light and Reflection

Create a maze in which light can travel indirectly from one corner to the corner diagonal from it.

Materials

shallow box with lid	cardboard scraps
mirrors	scissors
flashlight	tape

🔲 Ask

What do you already know? What do you need to know to get started? Where can you find the information you need?

_____

_____

_____

💭 Imagine

What are the possibilities? Come up with several different options.

_____

_____

_____

📓 Plan

Choose an idea. Draw a model and label it. Consider making different models for each stage of construction or separate diagrams of more complex parts.

📝 Plan

What are your steps? Use your drawing to guide your plan. Number your steps and write clearly so others can understand them.

_____

_____

_____

_____

✖ Create

Follow your plan to create your model. What worked? What didn't? What did you need to change as you went through your plan? Why?

_____

_____

_____

🔄 Improve

How could you improve your model? Do you need to start over, or can you redo a single part? If it works, can it work even better?

_____

_____

_____

💬 Communicate

How well did it work? Is the problem solved? Write a statement to describe how your model meets the guidelines of the task and why it is successful.

_____

_____

_____

🌟 Reflect

When might light need to be controlled like it was in the maze?

_____

_____

_____

_____

Name _____

Read the task. Then, follow the steps to complete the task.

Nature Notebook

Design and create a science notebook with a template for tracking nature observations. Figure out a way to eliminate having to carry it in your hands.

Materials

any items you choose, such as colored pencils, paper, a ruler, and string

spiral notebook
computer with word-processing software
pencil

Ask

What do you already know? What do you need to know to get started? Where can you find the information you need?

_____

_____

_____

Imagine

What are the possibilities? Come up with several different options.

_____

_____

_____

Plan

Choose an idea. Draw a model and label it. Consider making different models for each stage of construction or separate diagrams of more complex parts.

✏️ Plan

What are your steps? Use your drawing to guide your plan. Number your steps and write clearly so others can understand them.

_____

_____

_____

_____

✂️ Create

Follow your plan to create your model. What worked? What didn't? What did you need to change as you went through your plan? Why?

_____

_____

_____

🔄 Improve

How could you improve your model? Do you need to start over, or can you redo a single part? If it works, can it work even better?

_____

_____

_____

💬 Communicate

How well did it work? Is the problem solved? Write a statement to describe how your model meets the guidelines of the task and why it is successful.

_____

_____

_____

☀️ Reflect

Will your notebook work in other environments? Why or why not?

_____

_____

_____

_____

Name _____

Read the task. Then, follow the steps to complete the task.

Look Out Below!

Create a parachute that will allow an action figure to land safely on the ground.

Materials

any items you choose,
   such as aluminum foil,
   balloons, cloth scraps,
   wax paper, construction
   paper, paper towels,
   plastic bags, and
   plastic wrap

action figure or small
   toy figurine
string or yarn
chenille stems
scissors
stapler
tape

Caution: Before beginning any balloon activity, ask families about possible latex allergies. Also, remember that uninflated or popped balloons may present a choking hazard.

Caution: Plastic bags present a suffocation hazard. Keep bags away from babies and small children.

Ask

What do you already know? What do you need to know to get started? Where can you find the information you need?

_____

_____

_____

Imagine

What are the possibilities? Come up with several different options.

_____

_____

Plan

Choose an idea. Draw a model and label it. Consider making different models for each stage of construction or separate diagrams of more complex parts.

📝 Plan

What are your steps? Use your drawing to guide your plan. Number your steps and write clearly so others can understand them.

_____

_____

_____

🛠 Create

Follow your plan to create your model. What worked? What didn't? What did you need to change as you went through your plan? Why?

_____

_____

_____

🔄 Improve

How could you improve your model? Do you need to start over, or can you redo a single part? If it works, can it work even better?

_____

_____

_____

💬 Communicate

How well did it work? Is the problem solved? Write a statement to describe how your model meets the guidelines of the task and why it is successful.

_____

_____

_____

☀ Reflect

What helps to slow down the parachute?

_____

_____

_____

_____

Name _____

Read the task. Then, follow the steps to complete the task.

Light as Air

Design a machine to get a helium balloon that is secured to the ground to rise while you are 3 feet (1 m) away.

Materials

any items you choose, such as toy cars, empty boxes, marbles, paper towel tubes, and string

helium balloon with string
ruler or meterstick
scissors
tape

Caution: Before beginning any balloon activity, ask families about possible latex allergies. Also, remember that uninflated or popped balloons may present a choking hazard.

Ask

What do you already know? What do you need to know to get started? Where can you find the information you need?

_____

_____

_____

Imagine

What are the possibilities? Come up with several different options.

_____

_____

Plan

Choose an idea. Draw a model and label it. Consider making different models for each stage of construction or separate diagrams of more complex parts.

📓 Plan

What are your steps? Use your drawing to guide your plan. Number your steps and write clearly so others can understand them.

_____

_____

_____

🛠️ Create

Follow your plan to create your model. What worked? What didn't? What did you need to change as you went through your plan? Why?

_____

_____

🔄 Improve

How could you improve your model? Do you need to start over, or can you redo a single part? If it works, can it work even better?

_____

_____

💬 Communicate

How well did it work? Is the problem solved? Write a statement to describe how your model meets the guidelines of the task and why it is successful.

_____

_____

☀️ Reflect

What else might your machine be able to do?

_____

_____

_____

Name _____

Read the task. Then, follow the steps to complete the task.

On the Map

Create a map of your classroom or bedroom, drawing it to scale and including a key.

Materials

plain or graph paper
yardstick, meterstick, or
   measuring tape
ruler

pencil
markers or colored
   pencils

Ask

What do you already know? What do you need to know to get started? Where can you find the information you need?

_____

_____

Imagine

What are the possibilities? Come up with several different options.

_____

_____

Plan

Choose an idea. Draw a model and label it. Consider making different models for each stage of construction or separate diagrams of more complex parts.

Plan

What are your steps? Use your drawing to guide your plan. Number your steps and write clearly so others can understand them.

_____

_____

_____

Create

Follow your plan to create your model. What worked? What didn't? What did you need to change as you went through your plan? Why?

_____

_____

_____

Improve

How could you improve your model? Do you need to start over, or can you redo a single part? If it works, can it work even better?

_____

_____

_____

Communicate

How well did it work? Is the problem solved? Write a statement to describe how your model meets the guidelines of the task and why it is successful.

_____

_____

_____

Reflect

What was the scale of your map? What would the scale need to be to fit your whole house or school on a same-sized sheet of paper?

_____

_____

_____

_____

Name _____

Read the task. Then, follow the steps to complete the task.

Slow Down!

Find a way to slow down a toy car going down a ramp.

Materials

any items you choose,
   such as aluminum foil,
   carpet scraps, cloth,
   and wax paper

toy car
ramp or a large piece of
   cardboard propped up
   at one end

Ask

What do you already know? What do you need to know to get started? Where can you find the information you need?

_____

_____

_____

Imagine

What are the possibilities? Come up with several different options.

_____

_____

_____

Plan

Choose an idea. Draw a model and label it. Consider making different models for each stage of construction or separate diagrams of more complex parts.

Plan

What are your steps? Use your drawing to guide your plan. Number your steps and write clearly so others can understand them.

_____

_____

_____

_____

Create

Follow your plan to create your model. What worked? What didn't? What did you need to change as you went through your plan? Why?

_____

_____

_____

Improve

How could you improve your model? Do you need to start over, or can you redo a single part? If it works, can it work even better?

_____

_____

_____

Communicate

How well did it work? Is the problem solved? Write a statement to describe how your model meets the guidelines of the task and why it is successful.

_____

_____

_____

Reflect

What materials would be best if you wanted to make the car go down the ramp faster?

_____

_____

_____

_____

Name _____

Read the task. Then, follow the steps to complete the task.

The Best Nest: Design

Using supplies found outside, create a nest fit for a bird.

Materials

any natural items you
    choose, such as grass,
    mud, sticks, straw,
    and rocks

Caution: Before beginning any nature activity, ask families' permission and inquire about students' plant and animal allergies. Remind students not to touch potentially harmful plants or animals during the activity.

Caution: Before beginning any outdoor activity, ask families' permission and recommend use of sunscreen and/or sun protective clothing.

Ask

What do you already know? What do you need to know to get started? Where can you find the information you need?

_____

_____

_____

Imagine

What are the possibilities? Come up with several different options.

_____

_____

_____

Plan

Choose an idea. Draw a model and label it. Consider making different models for each stage of construction or separate diagrams of more complex parts.

📓 Plan

What are your steps? Use your drawing to guide your plan. Number your steps and write clearly so others can understand them.

_____

_____

_____

_____

🛠️ Create

Follow your plan to create your model. What worked? What didn't? What did you need to change as you went through your plan? Why?

_____

_____

_____

🔄 Improve

How could you improve your model? Do you need to start over, or can you redo a single part? If it works, can it work even better?

_____

_____

_____

💬 Communicate

How well did it work? Is the problem solved? Write a statement to describe how your model meets the guidelines of the task and why it is successful.

_____

_____

_____

☀️ Reflect

How is your nest different from one a bird would build?

_____

_____

_____

_____

 © Carson-Dellosa · CD-104855 · Applying the Standards: STEM

Name _____

Read the task. Then, follow the steps to complete the task.

The Nuts and Bolts of Robotics

Using recycled materials, create a robot with a moveable part.

Materials

any items you choose,
   such as bolts,
   cardboard tubes,
   chenille stems, drinking
   straws, disposable
   foam, yarn, empty
   boxes and plastic
   bottles, nuts, screws,
   a screwdriver, and
   wood scraps

glue
scissors
stapler
tape

 Ask

What do you already know? What do you need to know to get started? Where can you find the information you need?

_____

_____

_____

Imagine

What are the possibilities? Come up with several different options.

_____

_____

_____

Plan

Choose an idea. Draw a model and label it. Consider making different models for each stage of construction or separate diagrams of more complex parts.

▨ Plan

What are your steps? Use your drawing to guide your plan. Number your steps and write clearly so others can understand them.

_____

_____

_____

✂ Create

Follow your plan to create your model. What worked? What didn't? What did you need to change as you went through your plan? Why?

_____

_____

_____

↻ Improve

How could you improve your model? Do you need to start over, or can you redo a single part? If it works, can it work even better?

_____

_____

_____

💬 Communicate

How well did it work? Is the problem solved? Write a statement to describe how your model meets the guidelines of the task and why it is successful.

_____

_____

_____

☀ Reflect

How could your robot be adapted for use in the real world?

_____

_____

_____

_____

Name _____

Read the task. Then, follow the steps to complete the task.

Itty-Bitty Bag

Figure out the best way to fold a plastic grocery bag so that it is as compact as possible.

Materials

plastic grocery bag   ruler or meterstick

Caution: Plastic bags present a suffocation hazard. Keep bags away from babies and small children.

Ask

What do you already know? What do you need to know to get started? Where can you find the information you need?

_____

_____

_____

Imagine

What are the possibilities? Come up with several different options.

_____

_____

_____

Plan

Choose an idea. Draw a model and label it. Consider making different models for each stage of construction or separate diagrams of more complex parts.

📝 Plan

What are your steps? Use your drawing to guide your plan. Number your steps and write clearly so others can understand them.

_____

_____

_____

_____

🛠 Create

Follow your plan to create your model. What worked? What didn't? What did you need to change as you went through your plan? Why?

_____

_____

_____

🔄 Improve

How could you improve your model? Do you need to start over, or can you redo a single part? If it works, can it work even better?

_____

_____

_____

💬 Communicate

How well did it work? Is the problem solved? Write a statement to describe how your model meets the guidelines of the task and why it is successful.

_____

_____

_____

☀ Reflect

Would you fold other bags (such as paper bags) the same way? Why or why not?

_____

_____

_____

_____

Name _____

Read the task. Then, follow the steps to complete the task.

Dirt Brown

Without using brown, create a shade of brown paint that matches a soil sample.

Materials

soil   paintbrushes
washable paint   paper

Ask

What do you already know? What do you need to know to get started? Where can you find the information you need?

_____

_____

_____

Imagine

What are the possibilities? Come up with several different options.

_____

_____

_____

Plan

Choose an idea. Draw a model and label it. Consider making different models for each stage of construction or separate diagrams of more complex parts.

📓 Plan

What are your steps? Use your drawing to guide your plan. Number your steps and write clearly so others can understand them.

_____

_____

_____

_____

🛠 Create

Follow your plan to create your model. What worked? What didn't? What did you need to change as you went through your plan? Why?

_____

_____

_____

🔄 Improve

How could you improve your model? Do you need to start over, or can you redo a single part? If it works, can it work even better?

_____

_____

_____

💬 Communicate

How well did it work? Is the problem solved? Write a statement to describe how your model meets the guidelines of the task and why it is successful.

_____

_____

_____

🔆 Reflect

What object is a color that would be difficult to match? Why?

_____

_____

_____

_____

Name _____

Read the task. Then, follow the steps to complete the task.

Balancing Act

Create a balanced mobile with 3 or more parts.

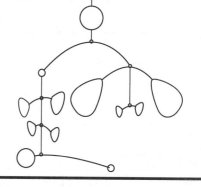

Materials

string or yarn
wire clothes hanger
wooden craft sticks
chenille stems

colored paper
cardboard or card stock
tape
glue

 Ask

What do you already know? What do you need to know to get started? Where can you find the information you need?

_____

_____

_____

 Imagine

What are the possibilities? Come up with several different options.

_____

_____

_____

📝 **Plan**

Choose an idea. Draw a model and label it. Consider making different models for each stage of construction or separate diagrams of more complex parts.

Plan

What are your steps? Use your drawing to guide your plan. Number your steps and write clearly so others can understand them.

_____

_____

_____

_____

Create

Follow your plan to create your model. What worked? What didn't? What did you need to change as you went through your plan? Why?

_____

_____

_____

Improve

How could you improve your model? Do you need to start over, or can you redo a single part? If it works, can it work even better?

_____

_____

_____

Communicate

How well did it work? Is the problem solved? Write a statement to describe how your model meets the guidelines of the task and why it is successful.

_____

_____

_____

Reflect

What helped balance your mobile?

_____

_____

_____

_____

Name _____

Read the task. Then, follow the steps to complete the task.

Aha! Invention and Engineering

Create an invention that solves a problem.

Materials

any items you choose,
   such as cardboard
   tubes, chenille stems,
   empty boxes, and
   yarn

scissors
stapler
tape

Ask

What do you already know? What do you need to know to get started? Where can you find the information you need?

_____

_____

_____

Imagine

What are the possibilities? Come up with several different options.

_____

_____

_____

Plan

Choose an idea. Draw a model and label it. Consider making different models for each stage of construction or separate diagrams of more complex parts.

📝 Plan

What are your steps? Use your drawing to guide your plan. Number your steps and write clearly so others can understand them.

_____

_____

_____

_____

🛠 Create

Follow your plan to create your model. What worked? What didn't? What did you need to change as you went through your plan? Why?

_____

_____

_____

🔄 Improve

How could you improve your model? Do you need to start over, or can you redo a single part? If it works, can it work even better?

_____

_____

_____

💬 Communicate

How well did it work? Is the problem solved? Write a statement to describe how your model meets the guidelines of the task and why it is successful.

_____

_____

_____

☀ Reflect

If your invention were made professionally, what materials would it be made from? Why?

_____

_____

_____

_____